### Written by Sharon Parsons

| Contents | Page |
|---|---|
| **Chapter 1.** *A Massive Food Train* | 4 |
| **Chapter 2.** *A Nutritious Diet* | 6 |
| **Chapter 3.** *Global Shopping* | 10 |
| **Feature:** *A World Of Food* | 12 |
| **Chapter 4.** *Food For Today And Tomorrow* | 14 |
| **Chapter 5.** *By Land, Air, Or Sea* | 18 |
| **Chapter 6.** *An Early Start To The Day* | 24 |
| **Chapter 7.** *From The World To Your Plate!* | 28 |
| **Index And Bookweb Links** | 32 |
| **Glossary** | Inside Back Cover |

# Checkout!

**Chapter Snapshots ...**

### 1. A Massive Food Train
How do supermarkets always manage to have such a wide variety of foods throughout the year?

### 2. A Nutritious Diet
We eat different foods every day to keep ourselves healthy.

### 3. Global Shopping
Look closely at the food in your supermarket. There are foods from all around the world.

"Supermarkets all

### 4. Food For Today And Tomorrow
Today, food can be stored for many months before we eat it. But why doesn't it spoil?

### 5. By Land, Air, Or Sea
Planes, trains, trucks, and ships transport foods around the world.

### 6. An Early Start To The Day
Supermarkets are not the only places that sell food. There are other types of markets, too!

### 7. From The World To Your Plate!
Take a trip around the world—in your local supermarket!

are large stores where food from around the world can be bought."

# 1. A Massive Food Train

Everyone loves to eat delicious food! Everyone knows that they must eat nutritious food! But not everyone knows where their food comes from, how it was grown or made, or how it got to their supermarkets.

During winter, it may be too cold to grow fruit and vegetables in your area. Why are we able to buy all kinds of fruits and vegetables in supermarkets all year around?

In this book, you'll find out how millions of people, animals, plants, food companies, and transportation companies are part of a massive "food train" in our country and around the world.

Many people work around the clock to make sure that all our foods are sanitary, fresh, and attractive. Others speed them to our supermarkets, ready for us to buy.

# 2. A Nutritious Diet

Every day, we eat different foods to stay healthy, grow well, give us energy, and help us think clearly. Most children eat a wide variety of foods every day:

- **Breakfast:** cornflakes and milk with a sliced banana; toast with peanut butter; orange juice

- **Snack:** strawberry yogurt

- **Lunch:** sandwich of whole wheat bread with lettuce, ham, and cheese; carrot cake; milk

- **After school:** cheese and crackers; an apple; milk or juice

- **Dinner:** tunafish casserole; mixed vegetables; lettuce and tomato salad; chocolate ice cream

# The Food Pyramid

## The Food Pyramid

The Food Pyramid is a diagram that divides food up into different groups and tells us how much we should eat from each group. We should eat less of the foods at the top of the pyramid (butter, cakes, cookies, fats, and oils), and more of the foods at the bottom of the pyramid (rice, bread, pasta, fruit, cereals, grains, and vegetables).

## From Wheat To Toast

1. Wheat kernels are separated from stalks.

2. The kernels are ground into flour.

3. Flour is mixed with milk or water, yeast, and other ingredients to make a bread dough.

4. Bread dough is baked in an oven to make bread.

5. Bread can be eaten fresh or made into toast. Yum!

What are some of the ingredients of the most popular foods we eat every day? Bread, for example, has flour in it. Flour is made from wheat, which grows only in spring and summer. Why are we still able to buy bread during fall and winter?

### Where Does Flour Come From?

Most flour is made by grinding wheat kernels into a fine powder.

Whole wheat flour is made by grinding up the whole kernel. White flour is made by removing the outer husk of the kernel before grinding.

A cheese maker checks to see if his cheeses are ready to be sent to a supermarket.

There are five main types of cheese:
- **Soft Ripened Cheese**—camembert, blue cheese
- **Soft Unripened Cheese**—cottage cheese, ricotta cheese
- **Firm Cheese**—cheddar, edam
- **Hard Cheese**—Parmesan
- **Processed Cheese**—cheese that has been treated with heat and additives

## How Cheese Is Made

Cheese is made from the milk of cows, goats, or sheep. Milk is mixed with a substance called rennet, which makes the milk separate into white, milky lumps (called curds) and a watery liquid (called whey). After many processes, such as heating, pressing, cutting, and storing, the curds become cheese. It can take 4 to 12 months for cheese to become ready to eat.

# 3. Global Shopping!

Where do the foods in our balanced diet come from? The bananas may be grown in Mexico or Hawaii. The wheat for our bread may be grown in Minnesota, the Dakotas, or Nebraska. Oranges for our orange juice may be grown in Florida, California, or Israel.

### The Spread Of Oranges

Orange trees first came from Southeast Asia. Now, they are grown in hot climates around the world. The United States, Australia, Spain, Israel, Brazil, and South Africa all grow oranges to sell around the world.

Even our milk may have come from a farm a long way from where we live. The tuna for our casserole may have been caught anywhere in the world. The mixed vegetables may have come from many other parts of the country.

We can choose foods from all around the country and the rest of the world when we go shopping.

# 4. Food For Today And Tomorrow

Food companies have different ways of keeping food fresh for a long time. Although the wheat in your bread can be grown only during spring and summer, it can be stored in huge storage bins, called silos, for many months.

## Preserving Food

Freezing is an effective way to preserve food. Ice cream was first made as a way of preserving milk in China 3,000 years ago! The first ice-cream cones were served at the St. Louis World's Fair in 1904.

In 1810, a way of preserving food by putting it in cans was invented. Some people call cans "tin cans." This is because the first cans were made of steel and coated with a thin layer of tin. Today, most cans are made of aluminum, which is lighter than steel and tin and easier to recycle.

**An early can, made with steel and tin.**

Bananas can be picked when they are still not ripe. Apples are picked ready to eat. They can be stored at cold temperatures for many weeks.

**"Use-By" Date**

A "use-by" date is usually printed on packaged foods. It is safe to eat food before the "use-by" date on the package.

We should throw out any food we have not eaten before the "use-by" date.

The ice cream and vegetables we buy may have already been frozen for many months. Being able to freeze foods means that we can eat them long after they have been harvested or prepared, packaged, and frozen.

The pasta in the tuna casserole may have been dried and stored in a plastic package for months. Some pasta is sold fresh, rather than dried. It is stored in a sealed package and refrigerated.

### Where Does Pasta Come From?

Pasta comes in all kinds of different shapes, sizes, and colors. We usually think of pasta as a food from Italy, but it was actually invented in China. Seven hundred years ago, it was brought to Italy by an explorer named Marco Polo. The Italians liked pasta so much that they created the hundreds of different varieties that we use today.

Some foods and drinks are stored in cans, jars, or bottles. Fruit can be bought in a can and jam can be bought in a jar. These foods can be stored so you can eat them many months later. But fresh fruit in season always tastes the best!

Putting fruit into cans in a canning factory.

Being able to store foods in a variety of ways means that we can eat certain foods any time we like.

# 5. By Land, Air, Or Sea

It's all very well having some of our apples growing in New Zealand, oranges growing in Israel, and bananas growing in Mexico. But we want them in our kitchens quickly!
So how do these fruits end up in our supermarkets, ready for us to buy?

**Did you know that a banana plant can live for 60 years?**

The next part of the food train involves transporting foods around the country and around the world.

It might take a couple of weeks for bananas from Mexico to reach the United States.

**Banana Facts**

Did you know that bats, not insects, pollinate the flowers of the wild banana that produces fruit?

Did you know that a bunch of bananas has more than 100 pieces of the fruit?

If you've ever left a banana in a fruit bowl for a couple of weeks, you'll know that it can turn mushy and black. Black bananas are great for banana bread, however!

However, plant scientists have discovered that if we pick bananas while they are still very green, they will ripen and turn yellow just the same as if we left them on the tree. So the growers in Mexico pick them before they are ripe. That way, they have extra time to get them to other countries where people want to buy firm, yellow bananas.

Fruit ripens slower when it is kept cool. Ships use massive refrigerators to keep foods such as bananas and apples fresh while they are transported across the oceans.

Refrigerated ships are also used to transport meat and fish, as well as other fruit and vegetables.

Some fresh fruits, vegetables, meat, and fish spoil extremely quickly. They are called "perishable" foods.

Perishable foods are often transported by airplanes. It costs a lot more to transport foods by air, so those foods are often more expensive to buy.

Some foods, such as strawberries, ripen a lot faster than bananas do. It can take only a few days for strawberries to become too ripe and start to spoil. If we want to buy strawberries during winter, they have to be transported quickly from where they are grown.

**Ripening And Spoiling**

Ripening is a natural process during which a fruit or vegetable becomes ready to eat. Spoiling, or decomposing, is another natural process where tiny living things work to break down the fruit or vegetable. Spoiling fruit or vegetables often provide food for the seeds inside each fruit or vegetable to start growing.

## Food Poisoning

Food poisoning happens when people eat food that has harmful bacteria living on it or in it. These bacteria can get on the food if we are not careful about how it is stored, handled, or cooked.

Microscopic view of bacteria.

Most of the foods we see in our supermarkets have been transported by trucks or trains. It is often easier and less expensive to move less-perishable foods, such as flour and sugar, by truck or train. Although the journey takes longer, these foods don't spoil.

Once all these foods arrive in our part of the country, we move onto the next stage in the food train: the food stores.

# 6. An Early Start To The Day

Early in the morning, truckloads of fruit and vegetables are transported from shipyards, airports, train stations, and farms to large and small food markets. There are many different kinds of food markets. In one type of market, fruit and vegetables are sold to the people who buy produce for supermarkets and other food stores. These markets are big, noisy places, where everyone finds out which fresh fruits and vegetables are available that day, and how much they will cost.

There are also special markets just for fish, meat, baked goods, and many other types of food.

### Processed Food

Laws say that the packaging of most processed foods must contain a list of ingredients. The list includes all the food's ingredients and additives. Often, these additives have long names, so canning companies use numbers to identify the different types of chemicals.

Companies that make things from fresh foods sometimes buy ingredients from markets. They use wheat to make bread and pasta, milk to make ice cream, and peanuts to make peanut butter.

### The "Pea" In Peanut

Did you know that peanuts are related to ordinary peas? Unlike peas, the stems of peanuts bend down and burrow under the soil. The peanuts grow and ripen in shells underground!

### Sold!

Did you know that certain foods can be bought and sold before they are even grown? This takes place over a huge computer network. For example, here in the United States, pork is bought and sold before the piglets are even born. In Japan, the cocoons of silkworms, which produce silk threads, are bought and sold months before the silkworms are born.

There is another kind of market for things that haven't even been grown yet. This market exists on computers and is called the futures market. People can buy "futures" of tea leaves, coffee, and cocoa that are not even ready yet. This means that growers know how much they will get paid for their crops before they harvest them.

### Barcodes

A barcode is a group of lines that can be read by a computer. Every package in a supermarket has a different group of lines to tell the checkout computer exactly what the product is and how much it costs.

Today, many products have barcodes. Even some books have barcodes. Look on the back covers of books bought at a bookstore and compare their barcodes. Can you spot the differences between the barcodes?

### All About Chocolate!

Chocolate comes from the cocoa (or cacao) tree, which originally grew around the Amazon River in South America. Chocolate was first used as a drink. During the 1700s, chocolate candy bars were invented in England. A few years later, a man named Henri Nestlé invented a type of milk that could be added to chocolate. You can still buy milk chocolate that has his name on it.

Most of the world's chocolate is made from cocoa beans grown in a country called the Ivory Coast.

However, chocolate is at the very top of the food pyramid, and so you shouldn't eat too much of it.

However, if there is a flood or drought, the growers might not grow enough of their crops to sell to everyone who wants them. The prices may increase. People who had bought "futures" at a lower price can now sell them for a profit.

Just imagine this! If the growers couldn't grow enough cocoa beans to make chocolate for a whole year, how hard would it be to buy your favorite candy bar?

# 7. From The World To Your Plate!

For many people, it is not convenient or necessary to go to the large markets to buy bulk amounts of different foods at the same time. It is easier for them to buy smaller amounts at a grocery store or a supermarket. People know that they can find and buy everything they need, whenever they want, at these stores.

Many food stores are smaller than supermarkets and specialize in selling certain types of food. For example, some stores sell only fruit and vegetables. Some stores sell only meat, or bread, or cheeses.

Supermarkets try to sell almost every type of food that people might want to buy.

Supermarkets are large grocery stores, where food from around the world is sold. Instead of having to travel the world to find bananas, cheese, oranges, and other fresh foods, we can just take a trip to our local supermarket.

You might say that a supermarket is really a display of the different seasons, different countries, and climates all around the world. As you eat your breakfast, lunch, snacks, and dinner, you might think about where your food came from.

Your food may have been transported by ships, planes, and trucks from faraway places all the way to the food stores and supermarkets in your area. Thousands of people have worked to get this food to you, including the person who cooked and served it! Luckily, you have the easy part—eating it!

## Index

barcodes 26
bread 8
cheese 9
chocolate 26, 27
    cocoa beans 26, 27
    Henri Nestlé 27
coffee beans 26
countries: Australia 10; Brazil 10; China 14, 16; Israel 10; Italy 10, 16; Ivory Coast 27; Japan 26; Mexico 10, 18, 19, 27; New Zealand 10, 18; South Africa 10; Spain 10; United States, 18, 19, 26
flour 8
food poisoning 23
Food Pyramid 7
fruit 20
    apples 15, 18
    bananas 10, 15, 18–19, 22
    oranges 10, 18
    strawberries 22
futures market 26
ice cream 14, 15
Marco Polo 16
markets 23–26
pasta 16
peanuts 25
perishable foods 20–21, 23
pork 26
preserving food 14–17
    bottles 17
    cans 14, 17
    freezing 14, 15
    jars 17
refrigerated ships 20
processed food 25
ripening 19, 20, 22
silk 26
silos 14
spoiling 22
states 10
    California 10
    the Dakotas 10
    Florida 10
    Hawaii 10
    Minnesota 10
    Nebraska 10
tea leaves 26
use-by date 15
wheat 8, 10, 14, 23

## Checkout!

More Bookweb books about foods from around the world!

**Inspector Grub And The Gourmet Mystery**—Fiction

**Taste Bud Travels**—Nonfiction

And here's a book about how a food allergy makes French ballet dancers very ill:

**Understudies**—Fiction

**Key To Bookweb Fact Boxes**
☐ Arts
☐ Health
☐ Science
☐ Social Studies
☐ Technology